Counting the Cost of Faith

Straight talk about deciding
to follow Jesus

Roger Shenk
Sarasota, Florida

COUNTING THE COST OF FAITH by Roger Shenk
4041 Bahia Vista Street
Sarasota, FL 34232
www.rogershenk.com

All scripture quotations, unless otherwise indicated, are taken from the HOLY BIBLE, NEW INTERNATIONAL VERSION®. NIV®. Copyright © 1973, 1978, 1984, 2011 by Biblica, Inc. Used by permission of Zondervan. All rights reserved.

With love for my family and friends.

Contents

Preface

As a pastor of a local church I am frequently friends with people who neither reject nor embrace my faith. They live someplace in between. Sometimes it feels like they're stuck there, not sure whether to jump in or jump out. I have often wanted a little book to give them that would help them count the costs and benefits of following Jesus.

This is that little book.

If you are not yet a follower of Jesus, please use these pages to consider whether it's time to take that step. Read it thoughtfully, and even prayerfully. God is listening.

If you have already taken that step of faith, read this to refresh your faith and to renew your understanding about the costs and rewards of following Jesus. And use this to help *your* friends figure out whether your faith should be theirs.

Introduction

I'm sorry if you've ever felt like you were someone's spiritual project—like they had to "close the sale" with you.

This book is written to help you decide whether you should follow Jesus or not. I believe, without exception, that everyone is better off when they do. But I also believe, without exception, that those who only *experiment* with following Jesus will find it to be just another religion that frustrates their lives for a while.

My promise to you is that this book will help you think through the costs and benefits of following Jesus—without being condescending. I'll be upfront with you that I believe there is a huge pay-off for following Jesus, but I also know that, in some ways, there is a considerable cost.

I'm honored that you would take the time to read through this little book, and to count the cost for yourself, as you work through this basic question of faith: *Should I stay where I am, or should I go forward in my faith by becoming a follower of Jesus now?*

1. The Question

No one likes pushy sales people. Most of us have been in situations where we felt pressured to buy something before we had the information to justify a purchase. It leaves us feeling as if someone took advantage of us.

I've never worked as a salesman, but it's no secret that there comes a point in each sales relationship where it's time to "close the sale." This is the point where, as the customer, we have gathered enough information to justify our impulse to buy. This is the time for the sales person to give us "The Ask." If our confidence and desire outweighs our fear of making a bad decision, the good sales person becomes our friend by simply assisting us with details of the transaction.

But have you ever been in a situation where you were ready to buy but the sales person kept talking? I know, for me, if the person keeps adding new information, it reawakens my whole judgment process and actually causes me to put the buying process on hold. People like that aren't very good at selling.

Jesus wasn't very good at selling.

Among the many stories of Jesus's life on this earth, there is one story where he had the opportunity to "close the sale" with someone. The man came looking for information to justify his impulse. He was ready. All he had to do was confirm that the information he had collected was accurate. And it was! He had actually done his homework! He was an "informed buyer," and Jesus could have become his friend by assisting him in trusting God.

But the problem was that his information, while accurate, was incomplete. There was something else going on inside the guy, so Jesus moved him back into the judgment process.

Here's how a first-century believer named Mark tells it:

> As Jesus started on his way, a man ran up to him and fell on his knees before him. "Good teacher," he asked, "what must I do to inherit eternal life?"
>
> "Why do you call me good?" Jesus answered. "No one is good—except God alone.
>
> "You know the commandments: 'You shall not murder, you shall not commit adultery, you shall not steal, you shall not give false testimony, you shall not defraud, honor your father and mother.'"
>
> "Teacher," he declared, "all these I have kept since I was a boy."

> Jesus looked at him and loved him. "One thing you lack," he said. "Go, sell everything you have and give to the poor, and you will have treasure in heaven. Then come, follow me."
>
> At this the man's face fell. He went away sad, because he had great wealth.[1]

Jesus wasn't interested in just "closing the sale." He wanted to make sure the guy received the eternal life he was looking for. And, apparently, this guy had a huge obstacle that stood between him and faith, and since he hadn't seen that obstacle yet, Jesus pointed it out to him.

The guy walked away sad because he wasn't ready for what Jesus told him. He had some serious thinking and praying to do.

Here's the question for you: What stands between you and putting your faith in Jesus?

For this guy, the barrier was wealth. If it came down to eternal life or his wealth, he would pick his wealth. But the point of the story isn't that "money is bad." It's not. Some of us have almost zero affection for money. But for each of us, the decision to follow Christ is always a decision to put him ahead of anything else in our lives.

---

[1] Mark 10:17-22

What would be difficult for you to give up? I'm not trying to get in your business about it, but I bet you have an obstacle that threatens to make you walk away sad.

On the other hand, I believe you're reading this because you're asking the same question: What must I do to have eternal life?

Perhaps your conversations about faith have to do with how good you've been. Most of the people I know, including myself, are basically good people. And most of the people I know, including myself, are generally tempted to do things we know we shouldn't. For whatever reason, we have some impulses to do things we relate to as "bad." Some of those things may be in the "soft sciences" of feelings and attitudes we have toward things and people. Other impulses may be in the "hard sciences" of things we do. Most of us struggle to be the people we want to be.

But if you were to ask Jesus, "What must I do to inherit eternal life?" and he were to answer, "Be a good person," many of us would say, "I am!"

And then Jesus would say, "Good job."

But then I think he'd say, "Since I answered your question, will you answer mine? What would you *not* be willing to trade for eternal life?"

So that's the question I have for you. What would you *not* be willing to trade for a life that's filled with love, joy, peace, patience, kindness, goodness, faithfulness, gentleness, and self-control?[1] Is there anything that you would rather hang onto if it meant letting go of those things?

I'm not trying to back you into a corner with a question that only has one reasonable answer. I just think that is the question we *have* to answer.

Let me explain what I mean. I'll use a spiritual metaphor of sorts: an altar.

Many people set up an altar to God in their hearts. For the Christian, it might look like a little memorial to Jesus. It has a copy of some of his favorite sayings that they read every now and then. And it has some candles called "prayer" and "worship" and "fellowship" that they light once a week to create ambience. Every now and then they sacrifice a little pleasure or give a little money as a show of their devotion.

That's all fine, but the problem is when they don't take down the altar that was there before. This other altar is an altar to "Me." This altar looks like a little memorial to our selves. We all start out with it, and add to it as we go. It has a copy of our favorite sayings and stories: our attractions, ambitions, hopes and dreams—but also our fears, wounds, addictions, and anxieties. We spend our days at this memorial, memorizing the sayings and stories, being led and inspired by

---

[1] Galatians 5:22-23

them, doing what they tell us to do. And this altar to SELF has candles called "work" and "play" and "responsibilities" and "relationships" that we light every day to help make sense of life.

There's nothing wrong with lighting these candles or reading these stories. They are what make us who we are.

The problem is that these stories and candles need to be moved from the "Me" altar to the "God" altar. They used to be the focus of our devotion, but they need to become the gift itself. If we try to live life devoting ourselves to both altars, we will spend our days going back and forth between them, mocking both, and creating the opposite of eternal life: bitterness, disillusionment, agitation, frustration, mean-spiritedness, shame, disloyalty, recklessness and impulsivity.

Here's the question again, stated differently: What is it that you can't see yourself moving to the God altar?

If Jesus said to you, "There's still something set up at the old altar," how would you describe that "something"?

Is there anything right now that you would *refuse* to move from the "Me" altar? Is there anything that you would *refuse* to put on the "God" altar? And if Jesus required that of you, would you "walk away sad"? Is there anything that you would rather have than eternal life?

Obviously, I believe the best answer to the question is to reassign everything to God. So that's the question I'm asking you to work through: Are you ready to give up anything that stands between you and eternal life?

Dare to pray this prayer:

> God, if you're listening, would you start to make this feel more reasonable to me? If there is such a thing as "eternal life," I don't want to miss out on it. So, when it comes down to it, I would trade anything and everything I have for eternal life. I would give up my life savings if that would buy me eternal life. And I would set aside all the earthly trappings if it meant I could enjoy all the good and eternal things of Heaven.

> But!!! Isn't it possible to enjoy this life now *and* eternal life later? I want to do what's necessary —I'll pay the cost—but I want to make sure it's the right cost. I don't want to play the part of the fool here.

> I guess that's my biggest fear, so that's my prayer. I want to make a good decision. Help me make sense of all this because I want to know what to do for eternal life. I don't want to "walk away sad."

> Thanks.

2. The Reward

I f you're really thinking this through, I hope you're wondering: What is "eternal life" anyway? That's the right question because otherwise this conversation is senseless, isn't it?

For most people the starting point is a felt need that, "There's gotta be something more than this."

That hope may be a reaction to the disappointments, frustrations, or disillusionments caused by our own failings or the failings of others that have affected us. If so, we may come to the conversation looking for deliverance or forgiveness—for some sort of release. In this sense, eternal life is *new* life: the gift of being able to start over, of not being trapped by what has been.

Or the hope for "something more" may be prompted by a mystical sense that our souls have "eternity" built into them, but are trapped inside a land-locked, time-blocked fleshly dwelling for eighty or ninety years. It seems that, if we can *imagine* there is more beyond this life, there *must be more* beyond this life.

Eternal life is not a uniquely Christian belief. But Christian belief is thoroughly rooted in the faith and understanding that eternal life is our reward. Many have heard about "John 3:16" which says, "God so loved the world that he gave his one and only Son, that whoever believes in him shall not perish but have eternal life."

Eternal life can be described in several different ways. When Jesus talked about the reward, he talked about "eternal life," or "the Kingdom of God/Heaven," or being "born of the Spirit."

Jesus treated eternal life as both a condition and a place. To him it was not merely a figurative state of happiness or euphoria in the same way we would say, "I'm in 'heaven.'" For Jesus it was an inner spiritual reality (He said, "The kingdom is within you"[1]), but it also had the qualities of being a physical destination ("I go and prepare a place for you"[2]), as well as another dimension ("Before Abraham was born [two thousand years earlier], I am."[3])

For followers of Christ, the hope and promise of eternal life is a root hope. We are banking everything on it. In fact, we actually believe that, if there was no future reward, it wouldn't make sense to follow Christ.[4]

---

[1] Luke 17:21

[2] John 14:3

[3] John 8:51-58

[4] See 1 Corinthians 15:19

That's extreme, I know. But let me tell you how we get there.

The early believers lived with their eyes focused on this man, Jesus. He was their hope. They thought he would bring a new kingdom here on this earth to displace the enemy power that their nation, Israel, was living under. But then, like all the other "messiahs" that people had put their hope in, this Messiah was killed.

Their hopes died with him on a cross when, in full view of everyone, he gave one last yell, and with it his final exhale. They stared at him in disbelief as he hung lifeless on the cross. They watched as the soldiers started methodically making sure each of the cross-bearers was dead. They watched one of the soldiers puncture Jesus's gut with a spear. Blood and water poured from the opening. His body was emptied of the blood, water and breath that had been life. They watched as the dead weight of his body was lowered from the cross. They watched as he was given a decent burial. They watched as the government posted a guard at the gravesite to make sure no one broke in and tampered with his remains. He died and was buried, and those who loved him watched the whole thing.

They grieved his death. Sorrow gripped them.

But then, after a day and a half,[1] he actually appeared to a crowd of them. They weren't praying for it. He just showed up! He was alive!

He talked with them and he ate with them. They touched his hands and spent time with him. By proof of many witnesses, this man who was fully dead was now fully alive.

Did you know that he appeared, in the flesh, to more than five hundred people[2]—not as private, unverified "apparitions," but to many people at the same time? It was a public appearance! His enemies even knew about it, and they grieved it, wondering when it would all end.

Jesus visited with the disciples for forty days after his resurrection. And then, one day—and I know this is going to sound like make-believe, or just an illusion, because, just like when he healed blind and lame people and raised dead people, this was a supernatural event—while they were all watching, he floated up into the sky and disappeared out of sight. This time, those who loved him weren't surprised, because he said plainly ahead of time that he was going to go to Heaven. And then he did; he went to "eternal life."

---

[1] 1 Corinthians 15:4 says he was raised on the "third day." He died Friday afternoon, and by the time the sun came up on Sunday, he was alive.

[2] 1 Corinthians 15:6

He also said ahead of time that when he left he would send his Spirit to take care of those who loved him. And one day, when 120 of these believers were meeting and praying, there was a supernatural phenomenon—there was visible light, like flames of fire, which suddenly appeared over people's heads, and they all started talking in languages they didn't know, but that the foreigners around them understood. They were praising God. It was so powerful a demonstration that three thousand of those foreigners believed that day. And they were so convinced that they reoriented their whole lives around what they heard and saw that day.

But not everybody believed. And to this day people still don't believe. But I believe it's true because the people who told me about it believed it. And they believed it because the people who told them about it believed it. And each of us who has put our faith in Jesus has done so because at some point we received a witness that we perceived as credible. And so we believed.

I hope you receive my witness as credible. I know that I have received a reward. For me there is the earthly reward of love, joy, peace, patience, kindness, goodness, faithfulness, gentleness and self-control. I didn't always have these in the same way I do now. It wasn't until I heard and responded to Jesus's challenge of "one thing you lack," that I was given these experiential qualities of eternal life.

And, because of these qualities, I really do believe that this earthly existence isn't all there is. I really do expect that there is a dimension of time and space called Heaven, and that I will go there because I have experienced its qualities here.

We believe that Jesus is still alive, and loves us, and is actively involved in our lives. We believe he was raised from the dead but not to live out a few more decades in an earthly existence. Rather, he is living forever in a supernatural, powerful, fully conscious and fully relational time and space. We believe he started that way (as God) and is continuing that way (as God).

If Jesus is *not* eternal, we would be foolish to expect that *we* will experience eternal life. But if Jesus *is* eternal, the most reasonable expectation is that *we too* can experience life after death!

That's what he promised. It is essential to his message and it invites you to consider this most important question: Are you ready to receive the reward of eternal life?

Prayer:

God, whether I believe in the "Christian" way or not, I do feel like there is more to life than this. Will you include me in that?

That's my hope, so that's my prayer. I want to make a good decision. I'm willing to believe in you and I'm willing to believe there is a Heaven. Help me make sense of this.

Thanks.

3. The Cost

Some people will try to sell you on a false hope that if you "just accept Jesus" he'll fill your life with good things and get rid of anything bad for you. There are systems of theology built around the promise that God wants you to be rich.

I believe wholeheartedly that God wants you to prosper. And I believe that he wants you to be well. And I'm sure he wants your relationships to be healthy and filled with peace, and that he wants you to get good parking spaces. Well, maybe not the last one.

Here's the thing. God has already said that he is more than willing—he is actually *inclined*—to bring hardship our way to help make us into the people he wants us to be. It's not because he's mean. It's actually because he's loving, with a flawless perspective on what needs correcting, and how best to do it. But his love doesn't minimize the pain of the correction.

This is where I learned that from:

> ...the Lord disciplines the one he loves, and he chastens everyone he accepts as his son.

> Endure hardship as discipline; God is treating you as his children. For what children are not disciplined by their father? If you are not disciplined—and everyone undergoes

discipline—then you are not legitimate, not true sons and daughters at all.

Moreover, we have all had human fathers who disciplined us and we respected them for it. How much more should we submit to the Father of spirits and live! They disciplined us for a little while as they thought best; but God disciplines us for our good, in order that we may share in his holiness.

No discipline seems pleasant at the time, but painful. Later on, however, it produces a harvest of righteousness and peace for those who have been trained by it.[1]

There's a cost to following Jesus. God is going to treat you as his much-loved child—he is going to bring pain your way to help discourage dishonorable behaviors and to encourage honorable ones. No child likes to be disciplined. Neither do adults.

There's a cost to saying, "I'm in."

Jesus himself predicted that his followers would be reviled and hated and persecuted. He said clearly that to follow him was like dying to yourself. And lest we think he was just talking to those who walked with him before his execution, the story of the church is filled with people who did give their lives for their faith.

---

[1] Hebrews 12:6-11

But the reality is that you probably won't need to. The only cost you'll likely feel is the cost of your pride, and the cost of not being able to do some things that once made you feel good (or at least different) in certain ways.

When you decide to follow Jesus, you're deciding to reject sin in your life. Sin isn't just something you're not supposed to do anymore. It's something that violates your relationship with God. In fact, anything that God says not to do is sin if you do it.

When you choose to follow Jesus, you're deciding ahead of time that God gets to determine what's right and what's wrong. What sorts of things? If I were to list everything, not only would I feel prudish to do it, we'd miss the point.

Choosing to follow Jesus isn't about looking over a list of his views about different things and then deciding that you pretty much share the same view. He's not a political candidate. Following Jesus is deciding that you will follow him wherever he goes—that you will believe what he says to believe, because he tells you to.

Wow, that's just costly. That means you'll need to change your view on things. And not just in secret, but in public. You're following someone who requires that you do what he says. That's costly.

People will laugh at you. They will feel judged by you just because you don't do the same things they do. They'll say it's your fault that they feel "hated" by you. Some of them may be your family members and closest friends. You'll need to choose between them or Jesus. That's costly.

One of Jesus's disciples, Matthew, remembered when he said this to those who loved and followed him:

> "I am sending you out like sheep among wolves... Be on your guard; you will be handed over to the local councils and be flogged in the synagogues. On my account you will be brought before governors and kings... But when they arrest you, do not worry about what to say or how to say it. At that time you will be given what to say, for it will not be you speaking, but the Spirit of your Father speaking through you.

> "Brother will betray brother to death, and a father his child; children will rebel against their parents and have them put to death. You will be hated by everyone because of me, but the one who stands firm to the end will be saved...

> "Whoever acknowledges me before others, I will also acknowledge before my Father in heaven. But whoever disowns me before others, I will disown before my Father in heaven.

> "Do not suppose that I have come to bring peace to the earth. I did not come to bring peace, but a sword. For I have come to turn 'a man against his father, a daughter against her

mother, a daughter-in-law against her mother-in-law—a man's enemies will be the members of his own household.'

"Anyone who loves their father or mother more than me is not worthy of me; anyone who loves their son or daughter more than me is not worthy of me. Whoever does not take up their cross and follow me is not worthy of me. Whoever finds their life will lose it, and whoever loses their life for my sake will find it." [1]

Many have followed Jesus all the way, giving up not only their relationships for him, but their lives. As Christians, we believe their reward is assured. But that doesn't make it easy to pay the cost.

I don't know what you will need to lay down. But, unless you're already a specimen of human perfection, it will need to be something. And unless all your friends and family members are those perfect specimens, you will face ridicule. That's costly.

Are you hoping you can "make a decision" to follow Christ without letting your girlfriend or boyfriend know? You're hoping you can secure your spot in heaven without giving up your spot on earth? That's not going to work. In fact, that's why I'm writing this book: to let people know

---

[1] Matthew 10:16-22, 32-39

ahead of time that deciding to follow Christ is deciding to abandon your old ways.

Now, let's take a breather here. My experience is that genuine followers of Christ are genuinely more likable than people who are just out for their own benefit. Most people like people who overflow with love, joy, peace (I know, I know—I've used this list before, but think about it!), patience, kindness, goodness, faithfulness, gentleness and self-control. People like people like that! Don't you? People like genuine, transformed followers of Jesus.

In general, that is.

The exception is that people who are filled with the opposite of any of those qualities hate people like that. And if you follow Jesus, those people will hate you, not because you're mean, or even (necessarily) because they're mean, but because darkness hates light. Let that encourage you, but don't let it puff you up. As a follower of Christ, you're just a dark-hearted person who found a candle to hold onto that won't go out. And the longer you hang on to it, the more the "cost" of following Jesus starts to feel like "reward."

But make no mistake about it. Don't choose to follow Jesus unless you're also choosing to leave your old way of life.

Prayer:

God, I like to think that I'm the kind who can pay the cost for something that's worthwhile. I know many people have paid this cost, but there are still some aspects of that cost I'm not sure about.

I'd love to get rid of some of the things about my life. I feel ashamed of some of my behaviors. I'd love to escape those. Is there forgiveness? Is it possible that part of the good news of this faith is that I get to leave those things behind, too?

Here's my prayer: I want eternal life. And I don't want the bad things of my old life. I'll start by trusting you with the things I don't like. Go ahead and take them. Please forgive them. I'd like to feel clean from them.

Thanks.

4. The Response

We've looked at the Question, examined the Reward, and considered the Cost—and it asks for a Response: Yes, or No.

But I want to make sure you understand something. While there's a cost to following Jesus, the reward of eternal life cannot be purchased. Eternal life is not for sale. God's favor cannot be bought. It can only be received.

That's good news!

Here's how I experienced it.

I knew what was right and wrong. I was a pretty good person. Even where I was bad, it wasn't the worst stuff you've ever heard of. But where I was bad, I caused other people pain and created some unhealthy ruts in my life that kept leading me back down roads I had said I wasn't going down again.

I tried to get myself out of the ruts, and I would spin at it here and there for awhile, but I couldn't get any traction. So I would spend more and more time in the ruts, because it became more comfortable to hang out there than to do the hard, ineffective work of trying to get out.

Then my life crashed. I'm not saying I was a superstar of sinners. I'm just saying that relationships I valued were being wrecked by decisions I was and wasn't making.

Then, one day, I had a powerful conversation with Jesus. It was just a short conversation, but there were many conversations that had preceded it. It could be told this way:

> I had come to Jesus saying, "Lord, what must I do to find peace and victory over this mess I've made of my life?"
>
> Jesus said to me, "Confess your sins, repent of your ways, show your remorse, and start pouring yourself into being a better person."
>
> I said, "These things I have been doing but I still feel powerless."
>
> Then Jesus said, "One thing you lack: Give up! Stop trying to control your life! Give in to me! Put your faith in me! Stop trying to earn my favor. I already love you! Just stop fighting against me and let me hold you!"
>
> In that moment I gave up and gave in. It was so freeing. I mumbled about six words that don't really feel complete, but they changed my life: "Jesus, I can't. You do it."
>
> I fell to my knees, face to my hands, tears to the floor. I was released. His presence filled me. I knew that I was forgiven, and that I would never, ever, ever go back.

I could have "walked away sad." I am so glad I didn't because in that moment I was given a new freedom in life. I finally had power to say no to things I hadn't had much success saying no to. I don't know why I hadn't experienced that before. But when I responded to Jesus's invitation and gave up control of my life, I gained self-control. Crazy.

And I was given a beautiful love for Jesus, and for the people around me. I started becoming a better person that day, because it was coming from the inside out. He changed me by giving me eternal life.

Today, I'm still growing into that eternal life. I'm still filling up with love, joy, peace, patience, kindness, goodness, faithfulness, gentleness and self-control. And as I grow, I have this continual assurance that I made the right decision to stop staying where I was and to go follow Jesus with all I am. As much as it has ever cost me is absolutely nothing compared with the great benefit of knowing him.

That's my story.

And here's my question: What if you were to tell your story? How would it start? How would you describe it? Where would you be right now in that conversation? Is there a part of the conversation you still need to have?

Seriously! Will you do this? Take time to write! It's more important than reading right now. I'll start the conversation for you, and then I'll give you a few thought starters along the way.

I came to Jesus and said: _____

_____

_____

_____

_____

_____

_____

_____

He told me to: _____

_____

_____

_____

_____

_____

_____

_____

I told him that I: _____

_____

_____

_____

_____

_____

_____

_____

He said (says) to me, "One thing you lack: _____

_____

_____

_____

_____

_____

_____

_____

I responded (am responding) by saying: _____

_____

_____

_____

_____

_____

_____

_____

Today I am: _____

_____

_____

_____

_____

_____

_____

_____

Prayer:

God, I give you my life. I trust you with it all. I put my faith in Jesus to lead me in the way of eternal life. I receive your love and give you mine. Fill me with your Spirit, and each day with growing love, joy, peace, patience, kindness, goodness, faithfulness, gentleness and self-control.

I love you Jesus.

5. The Following

So NOW what? It's one thing to *decide* to follow Jesus, but it's another thing to *start* following him, isn't it? Or is it?

I've been following Jesus seriously now for over twenty years and I keep learning. And the learning process is part of what makes this thing so beautiful. Because it's not about learning rules and regulations, it's about learning to know Jesus. It's about putting my toes at his heels and going where he goes and doing what he does.

In one of his letters[1], the apostle Paul told the believers under his care to stop chasing new beliefs. He said to keep on following the good news they had received from him. He wasn't saying they had nothing else to learn. He was just saying not to go looking for other good news; the *best* thing is not always the *next* thing. In their case, they had accepted the good news of freedom but were being drawn back into a religiosity based on rules and regulations.

Some of us are drawn toward that sort of legalism. Others are drawn toward other things. But if you've been hearing what I've been saying, you have been receiving a simple explanation of the good news that gives freedom. It comes at a

---

[1] Galatians

cost, but it can't be purchased. It bears a reward, but it's already been given. Not everyone receives it, but no one is kept from it.

When I talk about following Jesus, I'm talking about following *that* good news—the good news that gives freedom and eternal life by relying on Jesus.

There are different ways to explain that good news. The Bible even explains it in different ways. Here's one way Paul said it in his second letter to the Corinthian church. Read it slowly.

> ...We are convinced that [Jesus] died for all, and therefore all died. And he died for all, that those who live should no longer live for themselves but for him who died for them and was raised again.
>
> So from now on we regard no one from a worldly point of view. Though we once regarded Christ in this way, we do so no longer. Therefore, if anyone is in Christ, the new creation has come: The old has gone, the new is here!
>
> All this is from God, who reconciled us to himself through Christ and gave us the ministry of reconciliation: that God was reconciling the world to himself in Christ, not counting people's sins against them. And he has committed to us the message of reconciliation.
>
> We are therefore Christ's ambassadors, as though God were making his appeal through us. We implore you on Christ's behalf: Be reconciled

to God. God made him who had no sin to be sin for us, so that in him we might become the righteousness of God.[1]

My greatest desire is to help you find friendship with Jesus and his Church. I believe that it's only in a church that you will find the encouragement you need. So, if you have moved into friendship with Jesus, it's vital that you also move into friendship with his Church, because it's there that you will be encouraged in your faith.

Prioritize three areas in your life:

1. **Community**: find a place where you can have spiritual conversations with others who are following Jesus.

2. **Worship**: find a place where you can gather with other people around scripture, prayer, and singing the songs of the Church.

3. **Service**: find a place where you can give your gifts of time, talent and treasure to the furthering of God's love in this world.

Then, start setting aside thirty minutes each day just to spend time with God. Just spend that time reading a Bible and talking to God. Many people are energized by reading through the Bible each year. Many prefer to just read it. Many people are energized in their prayers by keeping a

---

[1] 2 Corinthians 5:14-21

journal and writing it out. Others just pray out loud like they're having a conversation with someone.

Whatever it looks or sounds like, just read your Bible and talk to God! And get plugged into a church.

And then... just be yourself. But be your new self—the one who has traded the old ways for eternal life, and is being filled with love, joy, peace, patience, kindness, goodness, faithfulness, gentleness and self-control.

On the other hand, if you're still counting the cost, I respect your integrity. If we ever get the chance, I'd love to introduce you to my friend Rob. He took years to count the cost—not in open, ugly rebellion or anything. He was a good man: A family man with a believing wife and teenage daughter and young son. He watched his daughter get baptized. He watched his wife get serious about her faith. He wasn't a bad man but he hadn't given his life to Jesus yet. He was actively counting the cost.

Then one Sunday he gave his life to Jesus. I can't explain this, but as nice as he was before, he's a new man now. It's hard to explain but his face looks different somewhere behind his eyes. He's a follower of Jesus now.

There are countless stories that could be told about people who turned to Jesus and found new life. I believe this moment, right now, could be the start of one such story. This moment is sacred because God loves you.

Would you please make this a point of urgency? The decision to follow Jesus is the best decision any of us can make. And the decision to *not* follow him is the *worst*.

Eternal life is yours for the choosing, as long as it's still "today."

This is supposed to be a little book, so I'd better quit. Thanks for your time. If it was helpful to you, would you please let me know so I could pray for you?

And, more importantly, if a friend gave you this book, would you let them know, too?

ABOUT THE AUTHOR:

Roger Shenk is a pastor in Sarasota, Florida. He and his wife, Wendy, have two sons, two daughters, and one grandson.

Contact:
Pastor Roger Shenk
4041 Bahia Vista Street
Sarasota, FL 34232
www.bahiavistachurch.org
www.rogershenk.com